U CAN 2!

Patty A. McCall

Janet Gale

Front Cover Artwork Rachel Michelle Jackson

Photographs on cover by Rachel Michelle Jackson and Stacy Erby

Printed by CreateSpace, an Amazon.com Company

Published by P.A.I.N. Foundation, a 501c3

ISBN:1979588309
ISBN-13: 978-1979588300

DEDICATION

To the women, children and men that have suffered abuse at the hands of another. We hope the true stories in this book will inspire you, give you hope, and show you that you are not alone. There are friends, family and organizations that you can turn to for help. Please know that you are worth a beautiful life.

P.A.I.N.
Prevent Abuse in Neighborhoods
Organization is a 501c3
Non-Profit

CONTENTS

Preface by Janet Gale

I would like to thank Patty McCall for her diligence in seeing this project through in its entirety and the encouragement and support she has given others throughout the years I have known her. As her administrative assistant for the P.A.I.N. Foundation, I can say that we all have faced many challenges and had to jump through many hoops to make this all happen. There is not one of us that has not been a vital part of the success of this project. Together, we can reach many others who have nowhere else to turn. I believe us to be a strong team, full of integrity.

When I first met Patty, I was going through many struggles that no one knew about. In fact, Patty may not even know how much just her being connected to me has meant, as I am sure is the case with others on our team. I wish I could say that things got better in my life's journey, but that wasn't the case, circumstantially speaking. I had to become that Psalms 1 tree that stands in the storms of life and praise my way through many things. The only way anyone can stand through any storm is with God holding them up. I am so very grateful for the opportunities that have risen through this U Can 2! Campaign; to be able to make a huge difference in the lives of others through our U Can 2! music video and this book. Thank you, everyone, for the time you took out of your busy schedules to help with this project. I truly believe many lives will be touched as a result of the time you all took to write, to act, to coordinate, to film, etc.

Here's the thing, and I truly believe this with all of my heart..."The fall of a nation is every man for himself." If we are our own entity and don't attempt to ever reach out again because of fear of getting hurt and connect with each other, we will never get any better than we have been. Believe it or not, there ARE some wonderful people out there that still care and want to make a difference in others' lives. They are a gift from God. Not everyone is bad. That was my belief for years, that everyone was bad, especially after I had been bullied for many years and faced several types of abuse; then my father was brutally murdered. I hated the whole world and felt pretty worthless. I just wanted to die, that was, until I found Someone greater than myself and the unconditional love that was placed inside of me by Him. Is this walk without challenges and ups and downs? Not at all. We all have to start at square one and work through it and expect those seasoned, wonderful people to be put in our path to help us out in our journey, however that may look.

My prayer for every reader is to be able to turn over a new leaf with God's help. May you be able to trust again, to love again, and be released from those past bondages of abuse, fear, guilt, and shame that may have haunted you your whole lives. My dear friends, hold on and take to heart Psalms 119 through your storms and surround yourselves with others who have made it through. May you be blessed and begin or continue to be released as you read through others' stories in this book. Your past doesn' have to be your future.

Again, thank you, Patty and everyone for all of your time and care you put into this project that will make all the difference in the lives of our readers.

From left to right: Loretta Smail, Janet Gale, Patty McCall & Teresa Stone Morgan on the set of 'U Can 2 !' Video. Thank you Teresa for sharing Park lane with us and helping ladies that need jewelry to complete their outfit and job opportunity.

ACKNOWLEDGMENTS

Talk about a true friend!! That would be Carmen to me. I was a new person to Hollywood in her 40s. Not wanting to be famous, just wanting to be involved in everything to see how production worked. I wanted my mind to stay busy after a very hurtful, messy divorce. Carmen was a Casting Director that new my story of why I left Oklahoma to go to Hollywood. Carmen unconditionally helped with housing and had a part in getting my first speaking role in Hollywood which led to the opportunity to join the Screen Actors Guild (SAG). From the beginning Carmen had a passion to be involved with P.A.I.N. Prevent Abuse in Neighborhoods. She has written many short films for educational purposes. She also wrote the script based on my book "Unmasking the PAIN Within." Carmen and her family were like my extended family, watching football games and spending the Holidays together. Carmen is giving her time to layout, format and edit this book. We are looking to get grants to film the short films to help break the cycle of abuse with our youth.

All stories were written by each author in their own words.

Carmen, Charles Berg (Producer), Patty

Carmen and Patty at Unmasking the Pain Red Carpet Event in Hollywood, CA.

Patty and Dea

A Message from Dallas-Dea Caldwell

I am a Survivor of Domestic Abuse. My name is Dea Caldwell and a proud community partner for the P.A.I.N. Foundation. Having met Patty McCall many years ago through pageantry we found we had more of a bond than we realized. I was to learn she too had been Abused!

Through my work as a skincare specialist and makeup artist I have met many women and men in my journey that have confided in me about their own troubles and abuse. Having been an entrepreneur for a modeling and fashion company the road kept intertwining with a recurring theme, which lead me to helping women and children, whether from learning disabilities or abuse it was important that I did not sit on the side lines.

As people come and go through your life I was surprised to get a call from Patty saying she wished to meet up again. Suddenly everything fell into place. From our Introduction of our Fundraiser Event Fashion Show for P.A.I.N Dallas in 2014, then our event at Hard Rock Café Dallas 2014 we were on the map! I became The Dallas Director for P.A.I.N. We held other events promoting our cause.

 Today, I am President of the P.A.I.N. Foundation and we now in 2017 have a website: www.paindallas.org and have events throughout the year. Dress for Success fashion event, clothing drive for Genesis Shelter, Children's Event – Children's Advocacy Center for Denton County Coat Drive from 2015, to present. I am a Motivational speaker for events and can be reached at dea@paindallas.org

Respectfully Yours,

Dea Caldwell

P.A.I.N. Dallas

Dea Caldwell, Patty McCall

1: Loretta Smail

The story of my mom being murdered. What it was like to live in a home with domestic violence and the after

effects in my life.

My parents divorced when I was 11 years old and my mother remarried an abusive man. I also had a brother and sister younger than I was. Mom would tell us that he was raping her. I remember mom drinking alcohol to help with the pain she was experiencing. This was a country scene; we lived way out on dirt roads in a log cabin in the hills. No one knew what was going on.

At one point we would go see our mom on visitation every 2 weeks and we saw these prison bars in the basement of our home. My stepdad was locking her in. As kids being so young, we did not catch on to what he was doing. When we asked about it, he would say he was protecting her while he was at work. He put them on every window and door of the house with locks and would disconnect the phone. She could not get out.

When I was about 14 mom pulled really hard on us to live with her. We never would have went if we knew fully what was going on. At the time we were living with our real father in a stable home. My real dad describes what happened as he put the custody papers on the altar in a church service because he didn't know what else to do but give us kids to God. The decision was made.

Mom was given custody of us kids. When we went to live with her, my step-dad took the prison bars down, but she would still tell us that he was raping her. They yelled a lot and she seemed afraid when he would come home.

As a child I remember so many times mom would pack us kids and everything we could fit in the car and she would run from this abusive man, only to go back again because she ran out of money.

We lived in motels, apartments, and we had no furniture at times and slept on the floor. One time we slept on someone's covered porch. I remember times of having no food. We were hungry and remember using my 50 cent pieces my grandma had given me for learning scripture to pay for eggs and bread so we would have food.

We had no money to buy school clothes. As a teenager I remember going to school inadequately dressed and was often cold.

My step-dad had a painful history of being in the war and his entire group was killed except him, he worked as a police officer and also in a maximum security prison/penitentiary, so he had much pain going on in his mind. I learned later that he had health issues that had him on strong medication.

I remember him being angry a lot, one time he went into a rage and began to rip posters off my wall in my bedroom.
He took us to church on Sunday and even owned a Christian bookstore in the small town we lived in... and yet all this was going on.

This is where the story gets intense:

This cycle ended one day. My mom and all three of us children were sitting in the upstairs of our home. It was a log cabin so it looked like a loft area. My step-dad had left the house that day and was gone several hours.

This is where the story got so painful and stayed in my mind. The vivid memories of what I am about to tell you took me into a deep depression for years.

When my step-dad returned, I remember he came up the steps and with a very rough voice he said to my mom, "I want to talk to you". As always I found myself saying to them, "mom please work it out with him", because they would argue and yell so often.

I blamed myself for years that this happened because of me saying "please work it out". But if I wouldn't have said that, he may have killed us all that day.

They walked down the bathroom hallway into the bathroom. It wasn't seconds later my mom starts screaming! I will never forget the terror in her voice....

"Call the police, he has a gun"

This was before cell phones and our phone was downstairs on a wall, we didn't have time to call the police because he started shooting her in the heart over and over again...

As a 15 year old girl I remember the pain and trauma of running down the hallway to save her life... as shots are being fired I am opening the bathroom door. I could have been shot!

As I am pushing the door open, I watch in the bathroom mirror as my step-dad shoots himself in the head. As I open the door I am also pushing my mother's body out of the way to get the door open. I remember stepping over top of her and lifting her head, holding her as blood was coming out of her nose and mouth. I heard her choking. At the same time my step-dad was laying on the floor breathing heavily. Even though he shot himself in the head he lived about 8 hours.

I run downstairs screaming at my brother and sister not to come in the bathroom. I did not want them to see what I had just seen.

My hands were shaking so violently and I was in such a state of trauma that I couldn't even think to dial 911. The trauma was like 10 times being in a car accident; my hand shaking so violently. I held the phone and all I could do was scream.....I could not think clearly. The operator on the other end started yelling back because apparently I had dialed a zero. She was yelling back, don't hang up the phone so they could find your location.

My little brother took his bike; he was probably 10 years old at the time and sped down the dirt road to the neighbor's house to get help. At the same time my sister and I were on our knees in the front yard screaming, **"Someone please help us... please help us..!"**

Memories are hard to erase. I still remember it like it was yesterday, but Jesus has healed the pain of it in order to help someone else.

We were then taken to a small house to people we didn't know and as a 15 year old girl, I sat in a corner of a bathroom and all I could do was cry and rock in that corner for hours till my real father came to pick us up. No one knew what to say to us.

My birth dad drove 3 hours to come get us. On that 3 hour drive home, no one said hardly a word. I couldn't talk, I was still in so much shock.

I was also questioned by the police because my handprint was on the doorknob and I had held my mom. It was a crime scene and we were not allowed to take anything from it. I remember begging the police officer to let us take pictures of our mom for we had nothing to remember her by... They only let us take a few things.

They said there were holes in the bathroom door and they don't know how I lived unless and angel protected me. They said statistics say he should have shot us all.

From this, I went home to what I call... burying it under a rug. The only one I would talk to was God. I remember crying at our country church at the wood altar every church service. I would sit in the corner of my room holding a pillow, saying, "Jesus please hold me." I was terrified of men and would feel panic attacks coming on. I would never speak in public and hid every moment I could. I couldn't look men in the eyes. I had no self-confidence; I was afraid of everything.

This turned into years of depression where I laid in a bed as much as possible medicating with sleeping pills and cold medicine to take the pain away. Every time depression would hit me, I crawled in a bed in a dark room, covers up over my face....begging God to please help me.

The pain was so intense I wanted to take my life but I didn't want my children to go without a mommy like I did.

As time progressed.... My story changes the day I heard God say in my heart:
"I want to help you but you have to get out of the bed"

It was one of the hardest things I ever did, but I chose to get out of the bed that day and allow God to take me down a road of recovery.

My road to recovery:

When I look back, I think one of the greatest things that helped me overcome was talking about what happened. For so many years I buried it. It was there, but no one knew the pain that was going on in my mind. Thoughts of suicide, flashbacks, fear of the dark, and the fear of men consumed my life. I did my best to live a productive life on the outside.

I especially hid my past when I was a teenager, because I had the fear of being labeled as strange or weird. My friends all had stable, happy families. How would this dysfunction and horror story ever fit into normal teenage relationships?

After the murder of my mom, for some reason, I never went to counseling. It might have been due to the fact that it was years ago and times were different, but I truly think counseling would have been a huge key to my recovery.

In my adult life, after I married and had two children, we moved to another state. At first it was very hard being in a new place. We moved to attend a Bible College. At church, our pastor would talk about how God was good and it was the enemy that comes to steal, kill and destroy.

I use to blame myself for years, thinking I was in some way responsible for what happened that day, all because of one phrase I said that plagued my mind. I remember saying, "Mom, please go work it out with him." and seconds later he started shooting her. It would replay in my mind over and over.

But comfort and hope began to flood my heart as our pastor would talk. He would say things like "God still has a plan for your life". I would listen to him thinking, "How could good come out of something so bad? How do I get free of the pain and tormenting thoughts that consumed my mind?"

I would leave that church and crawl back into my bed of depression, but as I listened to the Word of God being taught every Sunday, hope was going into my heart. I always packed plenty of tissues in my purse; it seemed that preacher was always talking straight to me!

He said that when we give our hearts to God, we are in a whole new bloodline, in a whole new family! I began to realize the painful past I had did not have to come into my future with my children and m family. In my mind I drew a line.

At that time, I was on high anti-depressants; I did a lot of binge eating, and gained an extra 50 pounds on my small frame. When the pain got too intense I would simply take sleeping pills and go to bed.

One day in this intense sorrow, I went in my dark room, pulled the covers up over my head like I had done so many times before. A was my normal prayer, I begged God to help me. But this time, heard in my heart "I want to help you but you have to get out of the bed". You see, I had given into depression for so many years, it was a way of life. It was like my destiny was standing right in front of me. Was I going to get out of bed and allow God to help me? I can say with all honesty, it was one of the hardest things I have ever done, but I chose to get out of that bed of depression that day. describe it like my leg weighing 10,000 pounds.

I always thought when I prayed that God was going to magically zap me and everything would be better. But in my case, it has been a journey. God has been leading me and I have done my best to follow his gentle impressions. Have I missed it at times? Yes, and even went back to bed at times. But the cycle was being broken the more I replaced the depression with other things. Every time the depression would try to hit me, I learned how to be prepared and counter attack it. I began to walk a lot instead of crawling into that bed. It was huge for me to get out of the house during that time. I often visited neighbors, went to church, or went shopping. Positive choices began to replace the negative that was trying to pull me back into that bed of hopelessness.

I had tried to get off antidepressants so many times before with no success. It would put me in a worse depression. But this time, I had a knowing in my heart to get a pill cutter and take a tiny sliver off the pill at a time. I wouldn't take any more off the pill unless I had an impression to do so which was usually every few weeks. It took about 6 months and I was completely free of the medication. I encourage anyone thinking along these lines to talk to your doctor first.

I also started getting involved at my church. I became a greeter. Greeting others at a door would seem like a simple task to most, but to someone who has been in hiding, it was a step of faith. At first some of it terrified me. But what started as one day of greeting turned into 8 years. God used greeting to build my confidence again, and I am now able to look at people in the eyes, including men. Never underestimate the small things that God asks you to do. Another level of healing came as I interacted with people.

Another life changing moment was the day I felt in my heart to video my testimony. I had never done anything like this before and it seemed so scary and big. But I followed through on the prompting. I got a webcam and sat at my computer for 20 minutes telling my story on video for the first time, tears rolling down my face.

I felt in my heart to give it to my pastor, but I was so scared I held onto it for 6 months before I finally gave it to them. When I finally gave to my pastor, a ball started rolling and they encouraged me to share my story on stage and with their TV department.

I also became part of a worship group, and it has been great healing for me to soak in the presence of God on a weekly basis at that group. We are also encouraged to share in the group. I've been doing that for about 7 years now.

I have had several life changing moments. On another day, I was in my kitchen and it was as if God and I were having a conversation. In my heart, I was seeing opportunities I had missed because I feared so many things. This particular day about 1-1/2 years ago, I prayed a simple prayer that changed my journey all the more. I asked God to forgive me for any missed opportunities and asked him to give me another chance. I remember surrendering 100% to God that day and to His purposes.

From that day forward God has opened door after door and keeps reminding me of my YES. I have had the amazing opportunity to share my story on three TV programs, recorded the music album "We Will Stand" and the "We Will Stand" music video. We now have website and I have been blogging about my journey of healing. I have also been traveling and sharing my story. A talk show is also in the making where I will be interviewing others who have tremendous stories of overcoming.

I thank God for his constant and patient love for me and that He can take such a broken life and restore it. I believe surrender and obedience to God has brought me out. His ways far exceed our efforts. So many small things that others could deem insignificant, God has used in His divine plan to bring me into freedom.

My word of encouragement to you or anyone who has faced trauma or severe depression would be this: Reach out and begin to share. You are not alone. The enemy wants us to hide, but God wants to give us an abundant, joy filled life.

I encourage you to pray a simple prayer and commit 100% to God and take his hand. I believe just as he took me on the journey of healing, he will do the same for you. I personally believe we all have our own journey. The healing process could be different for you, but allow yourself to walk with God. Even if things are new, be courageous and step out as he prompts your heart, and know that with every step, you are walking in more and more freedom.

** If you are interested in Loretta speaking or singing at your church or event, please contact her at lorettasmail.com

2 GABRIELLA

Gabriella Jasso
White

I am Gabriella Jasso White. My hometown is Mexico City. I have been in America since 1997. I'm proud of crossing the border as I have always been under God's wings. I am a survivor of domestic violence and sexual assault, in which I broke this cycle of abuse on July 13th, 2008.

I met my abuser in 1998 at the end of my 20th birthday. After we met for the first time, he was extremely persistent thereafter that I accept an invitation to go out with him for my birthday dinner. I finally accepted for that first weekend in September on a Saturday;

I had turned 21. I remember him taking me shopping and spending almost $400 on me. It was as if everything I wanted that day was mine. I began to see him as a prince. He made me feel safe and protected. I found myself enchanted with him at first. He was just coming out of a divorce, so I was very surprised that he chose me to be his next girl, especially since he was thirteen years older than me. Little did I know that I would be his fifth wife.

I found out a little later that the only reason that he dated me was so he could have a "healthy little boy." In October of 1999, we had a perfect baby boy with a 9.9 APGAR score. That night, the director of the hospital came down to congratulate me. My first born child was the only perfect baby in the hospital that day. Little did I know that seven hours after my baby boy was born I would face the side of the man that I was supposed to be safe with. While I was breastfeeding, my husband threw the harshest words at me that I had heard that day. "Well, I do have a healthy pretty boy. Now it's time for us to split up." I still cannot describe my feelings that night when he told me that. Since, at that time, I was not legal in the country, he said he was going to keep the baby and that I could see him anytime I wanted to. I was devastated. I refused his offer and told him that only by death would I leave my child. We split up after two weeks and I went to stay with my family.

He came back, though and "trapped me" into a situation where we moved in together again. We were okay for a while, but we were never a couple. We lived in the same house, but far away from each other emotionally like two random strangers.

Later on, our second child arrived in May of 2001. He was another perfect baby with an Apgar score of 10. Very few babies reach that score. My husband was expecting a girl this time and was very disagreeable.

We were still emotionally separated. It felt like we were still miles apart even when we were in the same room together. The boys and I ended up living in the country house while my husband worked in Dallas. We barely saw each other, so we lost each other even more so; well, then again, you can't lose what you never had to begin with. We lived that way for about seven years, only seeing each other on the weekends which meant that the kids were with me most of the time. After a bit, it came time for me to get things right and get my legal status straight. I ended up having to cover for my own papers because my husband barely supported me in this matter. He never did want to be responsible for me in front of the HomeLand Security Process, which meant that while I was married to him, I couldn't get my American Citizenship.

During the years we were together, I learned to recognize his "other side." He was a drug user and a very professional con man; always playing the victim when he didn't get his way. He did this with not only me, but with everyone around us. At the beginning of our end, things were really hard.

He lost his job in the spring of 2008. This is when my real nightmare was moving into our family with utter destruction. The drugs took the main center of attention for him. I couldn't help him at all with overcoming the addiction that, everyday, was destroying our home. On the night of June 23rd, he drugged me and then sexually abused me. I survived that one, but, since I wasn't dead, he repeated the act again two weeks later on July 13, 2008. I can painfully remember at least eight hours of sodomization, abuse, and rape. What I went through during my nightmare, I do not even wish that on my own abuser. Only God knows my hell I went through that day. It was the last day of all of the torture and the first day of a long, long, freedom. It cost me the custody of my boys. Since I was not a legal U.S. Citizen, he won custody of my boys. When the National Director of Migration heard about my case, she came to me in person and apologized for not acting in time on my case.

I always say these words: "God doesn't put anything on my shoulders that He won't allow me to handle. Only God gives me the strength to support my situation until my last day on earth and I am then by His side."

I did press charges against him, but the jury never believed what I was telling them. I was a cold case. It wasn't until June 2012, four years later, that the State of Texas used me as a witness in a case against him for sexually assaulting his girlfriend. Even then, though, HE GOT AWAY WITH IT AND STILL HAD CUSTODY OF THE BOYS!!! I lost count of how many police reports I had against him for violating court orders regarding the kids' custody. On the other hand, I have been more than blessed to know such great authorities that I can always count on.

On June 25th he called me. This time, he kicked the boys out of his house telling me that "That was it!" And how he couldn't keep up with the boys and that they were mine, so I went and picked up the boys. Since that day, the boys and I have lived happily together. There was still one problem though. Legally they weren't mine, so I had to support my kids plus pay him child support, even though the boys were with me. The reason for this is because the judge gave my husband custody of the boys even after a trial where he confessed to kicking the boys out several times.

This year I finally got to become a U.S. Citizen. Now I have the same equal rights as my (now) ex-husband. So if you are reading this and you have been a victim of abuse, I want to say that I understand you, more than you can imagine. I know your fears, your loneliness, and your freedom seems to be far away. But there's one thing you don't realize: You are NOT alone. I can understand your pain. I know what it is like to look at yourself in the mirror, looking at all of those bruises and those scars. In my case, I never imagined that so much blood could come from me. The pain of those memories is always going to be fresh. I know for a fact, despite these hurtful memories, that the love inside of me for myself is bigger than any fear. Once you decide to leave your abuser, this will be the beginning of the happiness in your life. There are other people that are with me in this endeavor to be ready to help you. We are here to keep you safe, even from your own thoughts. In the midst of the battle of leaving an abusive situation, there are so many professional people that are able to guide you on a road to freedom. They will help you become you....to be yourself....I may never meet you, but I love you!

Here are some helpful tips for an escape plan should you ever need them: When preparing to leave be sure and have all of the important documentation ready. You may also want to take pictures of these documents and send them to your closest, most trusted friends; at least two of them. Next, learn your exits and always keep a window unlocked or keep something sturdy beside you if you need to break a window. Remember to keep your phone charged all of the time. Be aware of the main roads by your house. Always keep a trash bag with clothes in it for emergencies. Never confront the abuser, try not to stir him up. The last thing you need is to make him upset. Call 911 immediately once the abuse has occurred and once police are there always ask their names and make sure they give you a police report number.

Shelters for abused women and children are the safest places for victims. Please remember that you must keep the location confidential. If I can do this, you can do it too... the road is not easy, but it is not impossible. Getting out of the abusive situation has been the biggest blessing in my life. Now God has blessed me with the empowerment to help others. Regardless of your religious beliefs, always have faith. Faith that you will make it and faith in God will powerfully see you through. Faith, hope, and courage are always with you and me. My children, Stephen and Alex, were also a huge motivation for me. Don't EVER give up!!

There are different purposes of life in each one of us. Once you leave your abuse in the past, you will meet the new you...the one that's stronger than life. Remember that I love you. I want you to look in the mirror and say "I love you" to yourself now. Do it a million times if you have to. Remember that you deserve God's best for your life. Trust God from your heart. This is where you will find happiness within you. I really want to encourage you to write your feelings down on paper. This will prove to be a release and help you let go on your way to recovery. Here is a letter I wrote to my abuser. I hope this helps you along the way. Again, remember to write things down. – Gabby White

To My Abuser: You are choosing to hurt me. You are a very powerful human, but deep inside is someone who needs help. Within you there is a heart that needs to heal, so you can forgive yourself for all of the crimes that you decided to commit. I am one of them. I never hurt you. I never wished you any harm, any pain, or any ill will...Why did you choose me? When did you decide to be my abuser? Who gave you the right to hurt me? I never deserved it. My only crime was to love you and my fault was believing in the dream of having a family. One thing I never felt was responsibility for your own wrong actions and bad choices. Those were, are, and will only be yours.

I do want to thank you though. I want to thank you because now I know a woman within that is strong as titanium and a warrior without weapons. I know this lovely woman within now that loves life and smiles. This woman will never cry again...not like you made me cry. Instead this woman will only feel tears of joy and happiness...tears that God knows are from happiness.

I hope that one day you realize how much you decided to lose by living in the tragic, harmful, awful world of "abuse."

Gabriella, Dea, Patty

Gabriella, an advocate and friend of Dea was a model at a Fashion Event at the Art Gallery in Dallas for P.A.I.N. Gabby expressed her interest in speaking out against sexual abuse & domestic violence, as she was a victim and now a survivor.

3 RAFAELA

- I grew up in Mexico, in a very poor neighborhood. I was a victim of excessive physical violence, abused since a very young age.

Being the oldest of 12 brothers and sisters, I had a big responsibility on my shoulders, to watch over my younger brothers, and to be an example to them. I started working at the age of 12 years old to help bring food to the table.

-I lived my childhood in a home where my father was an alcoholic, and violent abuser. I witnessed many times how my father beat up my mother and my brothers. I was beaten up with such brutality that, one day, I just ran away from home at the age of 14 and never came back.

I preferred to be sleeping on the streets under a bridge or in the parks, than being brutally beaten up. I was so traumatized that

*every time I think about my dad, I get Post traumatic Syndrome. I
lived on the street eating garbage for about three months.*

*During the time that I was living away from home, I finished high
school, and at the same time I found a job working in "las
maquiladoras" a clothing manufacturing company in Los Angeles,
sewing pants and all kinds of clothing. Later, I found an acting
school in Los Angeles, CA where I lived in the utility room behind the
theater in the back stage. I studied acting for theater and ballet
dance in exchange for cleaning all the classrooms and doing office
work.*

*Three years later, I got married and procreated two beautiful
daughters. Our marriage only lasted three years. We got divorced
due to religious differences.*

*My second marriage was with a professional ex-boxer Ruben. We
lived happily for the first two years. He was also a very talented
upholsterer and soon I learned the upholstery business. I did
upholstery work for many low rider show cars. We owned two
upholstery shops in South Gate, CA.*

*Ruben started to use drugs and soon our lives became so violent and
abusive, to the point that he was arrested several times for domestic
violence. Each time he beat me up, my daughters called the police
and then he would get removed from the house with orders to stay
away from us, but he kept coming back, and I ended up accepting
him again. All he has to say to come back is his magic words: -"I
Love You, -I am sorry, -I promise you that I would never beat you up
again". And here I am, accepting him again and again. He never
changed, instead he became more and more violent.*

*The last time he asked me for a last chance, I let him stay in my
house. This was the worst error that I still regret. He sexually abused
my oldest daughter, at that time she was ten years old.*

My life made a 360 degree turn in a split of a second. The police arrested him and was sentenced 20 years in prison.

The employees at the upholstery shops stole the tools, money, and materials.

The social worker took away my daughters, arguing that they were in a big danger with me.

The divorce was eminent. The judge ordered to give my daughters up for adoption to other families. I lost my business, my home and my daughters in a matter of weeks. For many days, I slept by the doors of the social worker office waiting for the doors to be opened to implore with no success to give my daughters back to me. Devastated, I contacted the father of my two daughters and beg him to claim my daughters, and not to let the social services give them away. He immediately contacted the case worker and he was able to take my daughters with him; with the condition that, I would not get close to them. I was only able to see my daughters for one hour per week in a public place.

My health deteriorated to the point that I was not able to even coordinate any ideas, I was mentally lost. I was wandering on the streets like a zombie for many days, I slept under a bridge close to the freeway. I had no reason to live. Many times, I tried to end my life.

Eight months later, I was meditating in front of an altar inside a church. With tears coming out of my eyes, I implored God to give me the strength to continue with my life, and to show me the way to recuperate my daughters. As my tears dropped down my cheeks, I slowly started to feel my face getting cleaned up. I started to feel that strength pushing me forward. My internal voice telling me that I must recuperate my daughters.

I have to fight against all odds. Now I have to fight with the father of my two daughters, and against social services. I have to

*demonstrate to the judge that I was competent, I must prove to
them that I was capable to provide a safe place, and financial
stability for my daughters.*

*The first thing that I did was to receive professional help from a
psychologist. I was referred to a shelter for victims of domestic
violence, where I received the help and support that I needed.*

*One therapy that helped me a lot was: -When I was taking a showe
and while I was receiving the water over my body, I imagine myself
washing away all the bad things that are hurting me inside me; like
sadness, hate, resentments... washing out all the negativity away
from me, and seeing it go down the drain.*

*Another exercise that worked out for me was: Every time I look at
myself in the mirror, I said out loud:* -Ruben, I forgive you for all the
things that you did to me and my daughters, but I also forgive
myself for letting that to happen.

Little by little, I started gaining back my confidence and self-esteem
I began to eat better, to exercise, to meditate, and I even joined a
congregation in the church. After a period of time, my face looked
radiant, I knew that my daughters were okay with their father, that
must focus on putting myself back together.

I found a job in an accounting firm, I was able to get an apartment ir
a safe area, and I also went back to school to finish my college
degree. I was ready and capable to bring my daughters with me.

One year later, I gained custody of my daughters, and I got them
back with the condition that I must move out far away from the
neighborhood where everything happened.

My daughters and I started a new life together far away.

My daughters were my inspiration, they motivated me to change
my path of letting violence happen.

Thirty years have passed. Since then, the tragic sequels from those
years are still latent in our lives. My daughters have resentments

towards me. They are still blaming me for putting them through an abusive relationship with their step-father.

I only pray to God to heal my daughter's wounds, and so their kids won't go through the same thing they went through.

Raffie Castellanos
September 16, 2017.

BIOGRAPHY

Raffie born on October 24th, 1958 in Guadalajara, Mexico.

The oldest of ten sisters and three brothers. Raffie started to show her passion for the arts, music, theatre, dance, and acting at the age of eight years old. She learned oil painting, needle crafts, and embroidering through her maternal grandmother.

In 1982, Raffie graduated from Huntington Park High School as outstanding student. She earned several Master Degrees in Accounting, Business Administration, Film Production and Directing, Acting for Film, and Insurance and financial Advisor.

In 2010 Raffie completed her film production education at the Colorado Film School in Denver Colorado. Raffie wrote several screenplays, which later she produced and directed. Among her productions are: Free Spirit (2008) short film nominated five time at the student film show for best production, best direction, best special effects and best music score, What Color is the Wind (2009) short film, Dear Grandma (2010) short film, Sombrero musical video (2010), Two Paths Meet, Calling all Angels, and Anawak musical short (2014) not to mention others. She also produced and directed several documentaries including "The Legacy of Rodolfo Corky Gonzales (2007)" , The DNC 2008 in Denver Colorado. (Democratic National Convention), Apache Freedom Run Documentary (2013). In 2016 Esparza Films and Free Spirit Films joined ventures to produce a long feature film, where Raffie was offered the opportunity to produce and direct her first feature. "The Mexican" Screenplay written by Pablo Esparza and Raffie Castellanos. The film is an awareness for abused women, because it talks about victims of domestic violence.

On set of a movie

I met Raffie through a set designer Eve Castillo. Eve shared with Raffie about the Organization P.A.I.N. Prevent Abuse in Neighborhoods mission is to make a difference through Film on the theme of Domestic Violence Awareness. The movie The Mexican has a scene where a victim of Domestic Violence is reaching out to a shelter, Our team of ladies are Advocates to help you find the shelter in your area.

4 JOANN MAUK

Let me tell you about not giving yourself over to one who will control you, if he will! My marriage had broken up 3 years before I met Johnny (name changed.) A friend I knew said she knew this guy, "who was looking for a long-term relationship." Of course, that tickled my ears! And yes, after meeting Johnny, he himself touched me with, "sweetcheeks", "honeygirl", even brought some flowers once or twice.....and then the downward spiral began!

Johnny liked his beer and later I found out crack! One on him was bad, but the pair of drugs was a nightmare! If I crossed him verbally, most times I didn't know I had, until his fist met my head. I was in for a sorry night of pain, crushed spirit and praying for his anger to stop. To STOP the agony and pain that Johnny wrought over me. In those fiery moments, I wished he would die! Sometimes, I even prayed for me to die! BUT, I was codependent on "having a man by my side," I allowed this to go on for 3 years. The last time was a friend of ours was getting ready to leave her husband.

Crystal (name changed) and Martin (name changed) had been married for about 5 years. The two of them and Johnny and I partied together only once. But, I didn't know how bad Martin treated Crystal, until she confided in me one day when we were at work together. She said she was afraid of Martin; she said he freaked out if he thought any other guy was talking to Crystal or just looking her way. She said he was insanely jealous. She let me know she and a friend at work, David, enjoyed talking and being friends.

Well, one day I come into work, and Crystal is not there. I found out that Martin and Crystal were driving the night before and that their car had rammed up under the back of a Dart Bus! Oh my God! He didn't! After talking with David and amongst ourselves we realized that Crystal must have told Martin she was leaving him. His insane mind decided, if he couldn't have Crystal any longer, NO ONE would have her. David was crushed because he had begun to truly love her. So the point of sharing about Crystal and Martin is that Johnny and I were driving our truck on I-635 near Mesquite on a Sunday about two weeks after Crystal and Martin's funerals. To this day, I can't recall what started the argument between us. But, all of a sudden, Johnny says," Do you want me to pull a Martin?", he slams on the brakes in the inside lane! My heart was beating so fast and I was petrified that we would be hit from behind. Gratefully, no one did hit us. But this incident shook my brain enough to begin to plan my exit away from Crazy!

It took a few weeks to start planning how I would do this. This truck, we were both paying towards it, but it was only registered in my name and I carried the insurance. So when Johnny was at work one day, I yanked my belongings into the truck. I had found a room for rent closer to work, we lived out in the country. I found a church home and began to fellowship again with other Christian Believers. This began my growth as a strong woman in the Lord. I was finally able to rely on, "I can do all things through Christ, Who strengthens me." With the help of the Lord and fellow-believers, I began to prosper in my Soul as I moved from being a codependent lonely and desperate to be loved girl into a woman dependent on the love and approval of the One Who truly loves me.! I am now strong enough to encourage other women to be loosened from the bondage of living in abusive relationships and truly begin to live Freely!

Dea McDaniel Caldwell and JoAnn Mauk

5 JUDY ANN

Unbroken (Excerpt)
By Judy Ann

At the age of sixteen, I was diagnosed with Severe Ulcerative Colitis. Up until then, I had a pretty healthy childhood. I was raised in a Christian home and was brought up in Christ's Love. In high school, once diagnosed with UC, it became very difficult. I was bullied in the halls for having to use the restrooms often because of the disease. I was always underweight and was teased for this. I still had dreams that I believed in. I loved Art and Photography and wanted to pursue it. I was in and out of hospitals and it was very hard for me as a teenager. I could no longer function normally and felt my dreams fall to pieces. My struggle to digest food and stay alive became my only option. I started working at this time and it was so hard with the disease. I needed money to save for my future doctor care. One thing I remember, is my faith and how Christ gave me peace in every hospital room. I remember crying out to Jesus in one of the most painful procedures and feeling his peace over me. It was just like someone had thrown a warm blanket over me. I then realized Jesus was my own personal savior. I finally knew what it was to have a relationship with Christ.

At the time I was suffering from UC, I was molested. I was 16 and emotionally broken. I had never told anyone. It created a deep pain in my heart for many years. I suffered deep depression and always cried out to Jesus to comfort me. I continued through high school but I spent all my breaks and lunches in bathrooms alone hiding from the ridicule in the halls. It was a very hard time in my life as a young teen. It was then that I began writing my pain and thoughts down. It was then that poetry came pouring from my heart.

After high school graduation, I was introduced to someone who I would later marry. We had met through a friend in a Bible Study group. We enjoyed each other and dated for two years. I saw no red flags at that time, so I felt for the first time someone loved me for who I was. We both loved the Lord very much and I thought I was truly happy. I felt accepted and loved.

When I had turned 20, the man who I thought loved me asked me to marry him. I said yes. At the time I was working at a clothing store in the mall. We were married the following year. I continued to work and save because I wanted to buy a home and have children. I had always wanted a family of my own since I was a young girl, so I felt so thankful.

In the first year of our marriage I started to notice things. I would often see my husband in the food court across from my shop waiting for my break. I would meet him and we would eat. He then would ask who it was that I was talking to in the store. There were often male shoppers, and modeling scouts that would come up to me and ask if I was interested in modeling. He had seen a man come in and talk to me and I told him about it. He wasn't happy with that. When I had graduated high school, I had wanted to model. I loved fashion and I loved photography. I wanted to be in front or behind a camera and modeling was so full of art and stories to me. I had dreamed of modeling and using photography to create art. But my husband seemed very jealous at this time and it scared me. I realized I would not be able to pursue such a dream. We would go out and I would get a compliment on my eyes and he was irritated. He would want me home most of the day while he was at work if I was not working. He started calling my work regularly asking when I would be home. One day I had gone out to my car after work, and found he had kicked in my car door. Countless foot dents covering it. I figured he had seen a male customer in my store talking to me that day about his purchase. I started to get very ill with UC again. The stress caused terrible flares where I would bleed for days. I was not sure what to do, so I just took it one day at a time. I soon had to quit my job from the fear and form my health failing.

At the age of twenty-five I became pregnant, with my miracle, my son Joshua. I had prayed and prayed that God would allow me to have a child. At this time, my husband was raging at me a lot, angry about life and things that were out of his control. He was calling me names and stating that I was ugly. It hurt deeply. I began taking walks and praying to Jesus to give me the strength to endure the pain in my heart. We were not doing good financially, and my husband had lost jobs. His anger was getting worse. When I found out I was pregnant all he could say is it had better be a boy. I had to take Lamaze classes alone or with my parents. I had always thought I would have a husband care for me and be so happy when I was pregnant. Not the case for me. I felt so depressed, so lonely. I continually cried out to Jesus in my deep depression. The joy I had in knowing I would have this beautiful miracle, my baby, kept me believing and hoping.

During my pregnancy, my husband starting raging and grabbing me. At one point he pushed me down very hard. That was the night I started bleeding and went into labor. I cried and cried begging God to not let anything be wrong with my baby. I was driven to the hospital with no assurance or love. All I could hope for is my baby to be ok. I prayed and prayed. I knew God was with me and that He would protect my baby. God allowed this miracle in my womb, so I just knew all would be ok. Even when at my lowest I remembered God still had plans for me (Jeremiah 29:11). And my child was knit together in my womb (Psalm 139:13)

I was in labor for quite some time, and I remember some heart issue, but we both made it. God gave me my beautiful miracle, my son. I knew God had a special purpose for my child, and I named him Joshua. I knew I would train him up in the ways of the Lord. He is a gift from God.

The time I had with my son was most precious. I was at home and spent so much time with him. He was a happy baby and my joy. My husband still raged at me and it was so hard, but I just focused on the time I had alone with my son every day while he was at work. It was peaceful and I was thankful for that time. I had met a wonderful friend and her daughter in our apartment complex. We took our children to the park and her family made us feel safe. Knowing that when my husband would rage there would be somewhere to go to get peace. At this time I had not shared with anyone what I was enduring except her. I somehow felt it must be my fault for marrying someone abusive. I now know this is far from the truth. Most who are abusive hide it very well until after they are married. It is what makes it so hard for us who live it. So many say, "Well you married him now you have to live with him." A woman is not to blame for marrying an abusive man. Most abusive men look for someone with low self esteem or have been hurt in some way. That was me in high school.

My husband started getting worse as my son grew. He demanded I keep my son quiet in the middle of the day when he would sleep before work. I usually left for walks with my son in his stroller. That began to make my husband angry because he wanted us home. I had decided to go to parks and the gym with my son in the stroller when my husband had left each day. Soon my husband would come home at any time for his break and find us out walking. He would rage and demand that I cook certain meals at certain times. He did not like me out of the house. I felt so trapped. I was sad that my baby boy was seeing his father call me names and push me up against walls. It was getting bad.

My friend in my complex became a safe place to go when my husband raged. We ended up there a lot. One night my husband had thrown a remote control at my head. I got scared. I called the police. They had asked if I had bruises and I did not. I was scared to press charges because I feared what he would do once he was released. I had to let it go. I continued to raise my son in my love and be the wife and mother God had made me to be.

47

It was a night I will not forget. It was also a night that made me stand up and leave. Courage was my friend. Hope is what I clung to. On that night, he said he would take my life. He said he would kill me. I decided it was time to stop hiding what was happening to me. I called my mom and dad, mom answered and handed the phone to Dad. He grabbed the phone and told my dad, "I am going to kill your daughter." When he hung up I ran through the house. I don't know how much time passed but the police were there before I could get outside. My husband sat on the couch glaring at me. The police asked if I was going to press charges. They made me feel like it was no big deal to have an abusive husband. In fact, they asked, do I really want to make things worse. I looked at him and said no. No, why did I say no. Because I was even more afraid that I would not have a place to go, or the consequences would be huge. My husband calmed down once he realized I could send him off to jail. That night I laid awake all night waiting for the light of day. My son was with my parents that weekend. I felt so alone. I was so scared, I just wanted someone to hold me and to tell me I will be ok, I will be saved. A few awful weeks went by. I filled my days with my son and keeping him happy. That is what was most important to me. And then it happened. My husband raged at me on a day I would not expect. He called me horrible names in front of my son, asking my son to repeat them to me. He slammed me into the wall, my poor little boy watching. He grabbed my son and ran out the door and said you will never see him again. I called my neighbor and they called the police. When they arrived, there began a hunt for my child. While they were searching the streets, one officer said, "Are there any narcotics in the house?" I said, "What? No way. Not in this house." Then he said, "Then you won't mind if we search?" I said, "Go ahead." When they arrived in my husband's room, we had been sleeping in separate rooms which was very hard to deal with, they went into his sock drawer. The police said, "Look what I found." I said, "What?" It was a tiny bag of white powder. I said, "What is it?" He said, "Crystal meth". I didn't even know what that was. He explained. He then said something to the other officers on the CB, and the next thing I knew they found my baby and husband. I grabbed my child in my arms crying. They handcuffed my husband

and took him away. That night my husband called and begged and pleaded for me to get him out. I was all alone in this, I had no one at my side. The house was empty and again I only wanted someone to hold me and comfort me. I lay awake holding my baby all night. The next day my husband's mom called upset at me for putting her son in jail. What he had been doing to me for years did not seem to bother her one bit. She had known that her son had pushed me down when I was pregnant. My son is a miracle to me. I cried all day. I had no one to get advice from. I was alone. I thought, how am I going to feed us, I was so scared. The next morning I let my husband out of jail.

I now had spent most of my time with my neighbor who was my friend, who I ran to continually when he would rage. One night I came home, he locked us out. He opened the door and spit in my face. I was humiliated as the spit dripped down my cheeks. It felt as if that hurt more than all the hits or names I was called. I cried myself to sleep that night. A few nights later, I awoke hearing laughter. I went down stairs and at my kitchen table was a girl in her bra and my husband weighing white powder on a scale. This was it. I had to get out of there. So, my neighbor's roommate who had been seeing all these things happen to me and my son, called his parents. They wanted to help us. They gave me enough money to get into a tiny bachelor apartment for the first month. It was no bigger than a small bedroom. I lived in that room with my baby, it was hard, but we were safe. I felt I had to do anything to keep my baby safe.

So we lived there for a few years and only had a tiny bed for my son and I slept on a couch. We hardly had enough to eat at times, so we lived going from food bank to food bank. I had a terrible disease which made it so hard to work and stand. I sold many things that I made so we could survive. We heard screaming in the halls every night. There were prostitutes and drug dealers on all sides of us. I took my baby with me to church every chance. It was harder than you could imagine. But we were safe.

As my divorce was becoming final, a close friend to me had committed suicide. He had just helped me move out too. I fell into a deep depression, but hid it well from my son. I went to church every chance I could and believed God still had a purpose for me and my son. And he did and does.

Since that chapter in my life there has been many other chapters, much pain, much healing, unbelievable miracles. Things I have written about in the hopes of reaching other women who are going through what I have. Hoping they will be comforted by knowing they are not alone. That God is with them. He is carrying them as He did me. Not long after this period of my life, I was married to an atheist, diagnosed with severe endometriosis, lost my womb and the ability to have more children, hospitalized with six surgeries, and still I am going through similar things. All I can say is, Ruin is a gift. We may be broken and in ruin at times, but God uses us and transforms us. It is when we are broken that we come to Him surrendered. We rely on Him. I know in my own life He is all I can rely on. It is like the Butterfly. The Butterfly struggles to get out of its cocoon, but it is in that struggle that its beauty is revealed. It's wings were crumpled but they expand with such strength once the struggle is over. I have felt broken in many pieces. God has taken those broken pieces and made me into one whole piece. Like broken glass that I place in my kiln. Under such intense heat, the beautiful colors in the glass are revealed. And the result, a whole piece of glass reflecting light and color. Just as my life being broken in many ways, God has used the broken pieces and created me to be whole in Him. I know it seems strange to say, but my brokenness, my pain, my illnesses, they have all been a gift in a way. They have drawn me closer to Jesus than I could ever be without those trials. So in the situations I am in now, I have seen my God move mountains, I have seen Him carry me, I have seen His Handprints on My Life. He loves us so much, that He allows us to go through things just so He could have us close by Him. God loves us, nothing happens to us without it going through His hands first. There will be awful things in this world, but that is a result of a fallen world. He will never leave us or forsake us. He has given us a Hope and a Future. Jeremiah 29:11 "For I know the plans I have for you," declares the Lord, "plans to prosper you and not to harm you, plans to give you a Hope and a Future." 2 Corinthians 5:17 If anyone is in Christ he is a New Creation, old things have passed away; behold all things have become new.

Tammie Starr and Judy Ann both live in the Orange County area of LA. Tammie and I have been friends for 6 years from when I lived in LA. We have stayed in touch through facebook. Tammie is a curvy, plus size model and such a strong woman of God with many encouraging posts with scriptures. I love her like a Sis. Tammie referred Judy Ann to be part of our book. Judy Anns story is very inspirational.

6 TIM SCHENKER

"I was very passionate after this religion called Hare Krishna. I would get up early in the morning, probably 3:30 or 4:00 and dress these idols. I would dance to them, clap and pray to them. I was very zealous and passionate after these idols."

Tim Schenker was born and raised in a Hare Krishna temple. Like many children there, Tim had daily chores. One of his was caring for the idols at the temple. But this wasn't India; it was West Virginia.

Tim's parents, Todd and Judi, converted to Hare Krishna after being introduced to the faith by a devotee in an airport. The couple then took their six children to the New Vrindaban community near Moundsville, West Virginia.

"One of the things that I remember from the ashram was that, most of the time, I was away from my mom and dad," Tim tells *The 700 Club*. "That was really difficult for me. All of the children from the commune would come together past a certain age. We would all live in this communal living. As a result, I was really lacking in that parenting bond." Tim also remembers a very dark side to New Vrindaban.

"Some of the things that were going on were sleep deprivation and mind control. Just a lot of domineering, manipulative kind of control over the people."

At one point, a disgruntled member of the cult took an axe and attacked the guru.

Tim says, "As a result of that, they hired my father to protect the head guru. We raised pit bulls to protect the guru, and he also had weapons."

When Tim's father discovered that some members of the cult were molesting boys, he threatened to expose them. But he never got the chance.

"We had a fire pit right outside the house there. That's where we burned all our trash. That's where they found his skull and femur. That's all they found. I guess the pit bulls had taken off the rest of the bones. That was really traumatic."

Tim's mother took the siblings and left New Vrindaban. The children were split up, and Tim went to live with cousins in Pennsylvania when he was just eight.

"Even though they were Christians, I was still a devout Hare Krishna. I did my Hare Krishna prayers. That's all I knew as a boy. I was sort of stubborn."

Tim's cousins shared Jesus with him and loved him unconditionally.

Tim continues, "This was the first time that I had experienced the love of Jesus in my life. It was totally new for me. At first I didn't react very well to it. I began to rebel, be stubborn, and throw temper tantrums."

Tim was also haunted by visions from his past.

"I began having really bad nightmares," Tim says. "Demons began attacking me in my dreams. They had long teeth and blood, very similar to the image of the idol that I had dressed back in West Virginia. I'd wake up crying at night I began to be so hopeless and even suicidal."

The unconditional love that his cousins showed him finally broke through Tim's fear and anger.

"There was a transition in my heart. I began to look inside my heart and compare my life. 'If Hare Krishna was so good, why am I so hopeless?'"

Tim also realized there was sin in his life and that he needed a savior.

"There was an awakening inside of me from God and from the Holy Spirit that I was pretty rotten down to the core," Tim confesses. "I saw Jesus, and I saw hope. I saw these people that had hope. I really desired that."

Tim accepted Jesus and began attending a Christian school. One summer, he went to a Christian camp in Ohio, where he was filled with the Holy Spirit. There he felt a calling to do missions work and later moved to the Tulsa, Oklahoma area.

Today Tim is a worship leader at Pryor Creek Community Church, and his greatest joy is telling young people about God's love.

"A lot of them have had no fathers," he says. "If they have had a father, [he was] not a very good influence in their lives. It is amazing to see how my life experience ministers so much hope and salvation to these at-risk youth.

"Even though my dad died, I have a heavenly father that loves me and cares for me. It says in the Word of God that He is a 'father to the fatherless.'"

Tim also shares his story with those who are drawn to eastern religions.

"There is a generation that is looking for something real. When they don't experience the real power and manifest presence of God in their churches, they believe Christianity is a farce. They turn away from Christianity, and they turn to these other kinds of eastern religions. I want to speak into this generation and say, 'There is a real God that you can experience, and He is living today. He loves you, and He wants to have a relationship with you.' There is no other, greater thing in this life than having a relationship with Jesus Christ."

Interview from CBN.Com   Randy Rudder-700 Club Producer

I met Tim as Janet Gale was recording songs for P.A.I.N. Prevent Abuse In Neighborhoods for Awareness. Tim and Nataly are the owners of Creative 4 recording studio in Tulsa Ok. Kenedee Rittenhouse is recording the song, Little Boy, that Janet wrote to give Hope and Healing for those that have suffered domestic violence. Kenedee is a very special young lady that I have encouraged since she was 16 at the Rising Star program. Our team is very proud of her as she is an American Idol hopeful!

7 TRACY UNDERWOOD
(SUPER T)

I remember one very chilly, but magical Alaskan evening when I was a child. The Auroras were out dancing across the sky and literally had the most brilliant lime green and yellows I had ever seen. I had been around these glowing lights since I was very young. My step father was in the Air Force and we had been relocated to Eielson Air Force Base in 1973. I have to laugh now, remembering what it was like to get the news that we would be living in Alaska! It also meant that I would soon be leaving a place I had grown all too fond of on Hill Air Force Base in the greater Salt Lake area. I remember having such an amazing grade school teacher Mrs. Abshire. She was funny, generous, kind and most importantly, she felt safe.

As I layed on my back in the homemade igloo that my best friend and I had built earlier that evening, I thought about what was coming the next day. The sky seemed much crisper that night, yet my lungs still hurt once the frozen crystals and -20 below air hit them. I thought, "Oh, how I wished that this were my last breath and I would wake up from the nightmare I had been living." Why me? What could I have possibly done to deserve this? Was this some sort of sick joke from the Universe? I thought that God was supposed to protect the innocent and his children. Nonetheless, all hell was about to break loose the next day and that it did. My life would never be the same.

From as far back as my 5th birthday, I had been sexually abused by my step father. During those same years, a neighbor boy who lived across the street, also had been sexually abusing me in front of his friends while my parents partied with his parents. All the while, everyone else in my realm was clueless about the horrors I was enduring on practically a daily basis.

These dirty, shameful secrets would haunt me for years, even though I tried to function and grow up as a normal adult. I kept thinking about all of those questions in my mind from those early years as to why this could have happened to me. I tried so hard to feel like I was "normal" by society standards around friends and peers.

In school I was in every creative, elective class possible and sports. I actually didn't graduate with my classmates. In fact I pretty much disappeared from school in the middle of my junior year. It all stemmed from the one decision I made that cold night. No matter what cards were about to be dealt, I was ready to tell MY TRUTH. Not the fabricated, lame story that was soon to follow afterwards and not to mention, full of malice and lies. Bottom line, I was being molested, violated and abused by both parents.

From the next year forward, I pursued the entertainment industry, made it my one way ticket out of hell. From about the age of 16 on I used my brains, talents and tenacity to escape the demons in my past and make something of myself. I would write about my experiences in my music, dream big about one day being a star, living in a mansion and living happily ever after with an amazing husband! I would finally be happy, loved, have a family! After all; isn't that what most little girls should dream of? Well, as the story goes, that never happened. No prince, no glass slipper. Yet, even now as I write this I still find some sort of humor in it all.

Fast forward almost 25 years later. I think, what a trip. If I wrote a book about my life, no one would believe the shit I have been through. Yes, I used profanity. (When and if my two children read this, they will laugh as they used to give me a hard time about how it was my favorite word). Sometimes there are no other words to describe what the hands of life deal. No matter if we bring them upon ourselves or they are just dealt by the natural pangs of life's journey.

Two years ago (2014), I was driving to Bend, Oregon to pick up my daughter. I reconnected with two of my dearest friends who have been like a second family and not to mention, a very big part of my spiritual story. I feel as if the more I write this, the more profound my experiences have been. I remember the drive back to Boise, Idaho where I live now and reflecting about that trip. The drive there was started off the same as they always did. Excitement because I was going to visit my daughter, it was always such a fun time. Lots of craziness with her friends and a ton of laughing! During my 4 1/2 hour drive, I would usually listen to all sorts of music on my playlists and sing at the top of my lungs. I would have visions of a new gig coming up, or just rock out. Halfway between Boise and Burns, Oregon it hit me like a ton of bricks. All of a sudden I had this overwhelming urge to just play random things on Sirius radio. It was as if I was being given a set list for an upcoming gig. I had no idea where or even when, but it was such a strong feeling. The songs coming on the radio were so moving, even mind blowing at times and a few of the artists, I had never heard of. As I drove all I could do was listen, write the names on a gas receipt and drive.

The trip home was even more intense. I made a playlist of all of these songs that had been "downloaded" in my head and started listening as if I were preparing for my next show. Little did I know, this was not just a show. I literally saw the marquee in my head and on it simply said, "The Calling." The second I had that vision, I had goosebumps all over, tears welled up into my eyes and I just started weeping profusely. I had just been given the answer that I waited my whole life for. All of these things happened because I had been chosen. As weird as it may seem or sound that was exactly the feeling. It was as if this huge weight had been lifted off of my shoulders. It was a truly a calling far beyond what I even thought was capable inside of me.

I realized, had I not gone through what I did, I would not have been able to talk about it and possibly help others in the future. I believe that we are all put through certain tests in our lives and they aren't necessarily because of a drama that we created. Sometimes, other people's poor choices are truly blessings in disguise. Maybe it is just how we choose to look at adversity. All I know is that this was one vision that became a very big reality in less than one year, but I had been preparing for my whole life and didn't know it!

I took the vision that I had been given and got back to Boise. The night that I got home I had one of the most profound dreams that I believe was no accident. I was sitting in the audience at The Egyptian Theater here in Boise. I watched the big screen and listened to the music. I remember what was the image of a man standing at center stage, but I never saw his face. It was a feeling. A feeling as if I were in the presence of God or higher power. The feeling was accompanied by speaking, but not in my ears it was in my body. I was watching myself on this stage, but someone else was controlling what I was saying and it was the man, not me, yet it was the essence of me. I remember crying, laughing having all of the emotions soar through my veins. It was all happening so fast! I felt so loved and nervous! What I realized, was the feeling. It was a feeling of being home and what I had been prepared for. Not only that, this experience was as if that higher power was making me experience all of the wonderful things that He had been doing for me. It felt like a warm blanket and I remember the reason I cried. Someone finally understood. Not only did they understand, the pain was shown to me in a way I had never envisioned. Joy! Pain with a purpose! I was spoken to through my inner soul and it was shared in a manner that told me this is how the audience and other like me would feel after this event.

After a solid year of countless hours working on video footage, gathering up my favorite musical "victims", it was going to happen. I still can't believe to this day it actually came to fruition. The Calling took place on August 30th, 2014 at The Egyptian Theater in Boise, Idaho. It was a success and soon after the Burns Paiute Indian Tribe asked us to come and do the exact same production. This time we actually got paid. Everyone that helped during the first one sacrificed countless hours, the donations were amazing and I learned not only what I was made of, but how great our community is.

So, you may ask, "what is The Calling really about?" Well, we all have one. Mine has been about sharing my story, experiences, accompanied by music and the creativity that surrounds my life in hopes that it will help others. This journey is far from over. In fact, it has just begun, but that's another story to be determined.

Tracy Underwood (Super T) has a very powerful music video "Save Me!" She entered her music video into a Film Festival where the P.A.I.N. Prevent Abuse in Neighborhoods gave awards for the. best short film, documentary, feature film or music video that had the theme of Abuse awareness. She won first place for the music video and a documentary the next year. Tracy is also a talented performer on the stage. She performs at several other events to speak out about Abuse!

SUPER T and PATTY at Hard Rock Dallas for an event for P.A.I.N.

8 RACHEL

Let me introduce myself, my name is Rachel Jackson; I am a singer/songwriter and speaker. My heart is to minister to people and encourage people to be real and honest with God, themselves, and others. My prayer is that through music and word will come healing, deliverance, restoration, and salvation. In ministering in this way a movement was started that has made a large impact in schools. I have been in ministry for 16 years reaching out to women, children, youth, and college aged students. My music has received regular airplay on several radio stations across America. I have lead worship in many settings from church camps to inside prison walls. I serve as a youth leader next to my husband that is the youth pastor of Angus Church in Sand Springs, OK. Jared Jackson and I have been married for 13 years and have three children.

I've been blessed with a life that lends itself to exploration and discovery. My greatest find during my journey so far, has been true friendships. The people who I am surrounded with strengthen my character and faith. These wonderful friends add immense richness and fulfillment to my life – making struggles more bearable and victories more memorable.

God is the center and focus of my ministry and my love and compassion for people has lead me to advocate for them through my singing, songwriting and speaking. . I never finish writing a song hoping to sing it alone forever. We all sound better together; we all "do life" better together. This is at the core of what I believe and whom I believe in: that we would be strengthened in community, joined as one and making a difference for something bigger than ourselves. This is what I see in the mission of the P.A.I.N. Foundation!

I typically do not talk about or dwell on my past; frankly it is embarrassing and hurtful. Recently I was faced with the fact that things in my past make me emotional. However, this is ok. I say that because if I ever become numb and lose the tears then the next question is; is my heart hardening? At no point should what happened be ok, so I let the tears fall, all the while remembering God is here and I am safe with him.

My prayer is that someone is ministered to through sharing my experiences and that healing will take place. I now identify myself with Christ and do not define myself by my past. I understand that some of my past pain has in part shaped me into who I am today and God has taken what the enemy meant for harm and he has done a new work in me to bring me to where I am today. So here I go!

I give Glory to God for my life and for the way he brought me out of destruction and death! I once was full of anger and pain. Now I have joy and peace! I once hated people. Now people are my heart's mission! I once found an escape in drugs but now Jesus is my escape from this world! There was a time I had no desire or purpose to live. God gave me purpose and I am so thankful for breath! I desire to thrive and endure till the end, and reach others and see deliverance and healing!

I grew up in a home where my Mom was a God fearing woman.

She loved my brother and me very much. I remember her saying things like... she would take a trip to the depths of Hell to pull me out and rescue me, with me cursing her all the way if she had too. She would be willing to do anything for my brother and me. I have so much gratitude to my Mom for always being there. Now that I am older and a mother myself, I see the amazing role she had in my life that made me who I am today. I am a fighter.

My father was not the role model my mother was, in fact he abused me physically, emotionally, verbally and spiritually. He was also sexually inappropriate. I was an angry suicidal teen, desperate for help, not knowing who I was. The interesting twist to this story, which should be a shock, but sadly in today's world, isn't, is my father was a minister. As a young child my parents were missionaries and church planters in Mexico for two and a half years. We saw God do amazing works, miracles that changed whole communities. At the same time my father, who claimed to serve God, condemned the rest of us in the family. He was very controlling and used the Bible as a tool to manipulate, confuse and accuse. He attempted to kill my mother in front of me and my brother, for what reason, I still don't understand today. I would often say to him, "whatever God you serve I will NEVER have anything to do with!" There were times I thought that God wasn't real but if he was.... he must hate me. I was told often I was the devil's child and my rebellion and dishonor would cause me an early death, which as a young girl, I interpreted, as he wanted me dead.

My mother stood strong and kept faith but was wore out at the same time. She was scared to leave due to his threats and weird ways. My dad had isolated her away from all family and friends in Florida and moved her to Oklahoma after the first year of marriage. She was very close to her father who died 10 days after the forced move. She hung in there and waited for a safe escape from the world she had never imagined would be her world.

As a teen I began using drugs. I hid my struggles from people and many didn't know the condition I was in, not even my mom. At one point, I hit rock bottom and was contemplating taking my own life. Then suddenly I was being asked to come to church by a friend of my brothers. I hesitated but decided to see if maybe this God I was taught about was different than what I had perceived as a child. My brother now believed in God like our mom did! He and his friends were reaching out to me. I went to church...I fell to my knees at the altar call and asked God to reveal himself to me in an undeniable way. Wow, did he ever and he has continued to be my rock from then on. I am completely aware that I am undeserving of his love and acceptance by any efforts of my own, but his love is unconditional and exquisite. I am a continual work in progress.

It has been 18 years since God gave me NEW life! He has blessed me in many ways. My wonderful husband, Jared being one, he love me as I am and loves God wholeheartedly. He has helped me overcome many things I was unable to on my own. I am a different person because of him in my life and I am very thankful. Then there are our three children. Doctors had told me I could NOT have children due to PCOS (Polycystic Ovary Syndrome) and also being Insulin Resistant since birth. However, my God is bigger than a doctor's report! Gavin, Aliyah, and Jovie are amazing and I am proud to be their mom.

There is so much more to my story, but most importantly, I know Jesus is real and I trust him with everything in me. He rescued and delivered me from my situation and healed me of the hurt and pain I made the right steps for healing and I will continue to give it all to God. I forgave my dad and continue to pray for restoration. Though it will never be what it should have been, with unconditional love and wisdom I'm open to having a relationship with him today. I am very close to my mother and brother and I am so thankful for my relationship with them. We all praise God who brought us out of all of it.

My heart cries out to the hurting. I desire so much for them to see there is a way out of pain. Jesus is the way, the truth, and the life. He is a definite light in this dark, cruel and dying world.

Rachel Jackson
www.racheljacksonmusic.com

Rachel Michelle Jackson and Patty met through her PR Carol Collins-Matza. Rachel's talents are many, she spoke and sang at the Hard Rock Dallas at our kick off for the U Can 2 Movement! She is also a photographer and the designer of the book cover for U Can 2!

9 FLORANCE

I am sharing my story in hopes to see other women overcome their struggles of abuse and obtain a new type of freedom about them.

I was raised in a home in which my father struggled with an addiction to alcohol and my mother faced struggles with psychological problems. At an early age, I witnessed the physical beatings of my mother by my father. I and my siblings would often hide from our mother, who would in turn, "lose it" and beat us with the buckle end of a belt while hiding behind a chair. I and my siblings would often have meals withheld from us and be locked in our rooms, begging to come out, until we wet our pants. We would then get a beating for wetting our pants.

My mom and dad's relationship was toxic, and my parents soon split up, got back together, and then divorced when I was around eight years old. Afterwards, my mom found another guy which became my step-father. My mother obtained a job that required her to work night shifts and leave me and my siblings with our step-father. That is when the sexual abuse began. My step-father blamed my mother for taking the night shift, attempting to justify his actions of sexual abuse towards me. The nightmare continued until I was fifteen years old, in which DHS stepped in and took me and my siblings from our home. Shortly thereafter, my mother signed her rights away. From there, me and my siblings went to live with our father, but I felt that he didn't want us either. At age fifteen, I found myself pregnant, haunted by the devastation of the abuse I had suffered. When I was sixteen, I gave birth to my first child, and I have been on my own ever since that time. I found myself always searching for my mother's approval and always longing for love from her. It plagued my life for many years. Tearfully, I would often reminisce about the feelings of abandonment and rejection I went through. Up until my mother passed away, my mother still held tight to the idea that she would always choose her husband over her kids. My only saving grace was God's love. That's Who got me through. My first, second, and third marriage turned violent, inadvertently not realizing that I "sought out" those types of relationships because it was all I had ever known my whole life. I once went to a psychiatrist that pointed out the problem. "You ask to be beat," he told me. "Your defensive, fighting behavior is all you have known and in turn you are asking to be beat." I admit I thought he was crazy, but later I understood what he was saying. When someone has been raised in and surrounded with a strife-filled environment all of their life, that's all they know. I realize now that breaking the cycle of abuse is not easy. I had to learn to recognize the rage inside myself to be able to take the first steps of overcoming and breaking this abuse cycle. Facing depression, anxiety, PTSD, and time in the ICU from kidney failure has been an uphill battle for me. I remember a time in my life where I was mad at God for "forcing" me to live. I could not "feel" any emotions, even if someone sincerely cared for me."

I attribute my process of recovery to God, my daughter, and Al Anon. I am able to accept myself, smile more freely, and experience whole new doors of opportunity in my life towards freedom that God has given to me. Some advice that I would give to someone who has walked in similar shoes is, "This journey to recovery is a process that doesn't happen overnight, but if you keep plugging away at it, you will see God guide you through to a wonderful destiny. You ARE very valuable and God loves you very, very much. Don't ever give up."

Remember, the winners are not the perfect people, but the ones who keep getting back up and keep on going." -*Florance Paad Johnson*

Excerpt

"Her Own Life Story." 2016.

Florance and Patty after a makeover from BBB Body Beauty and Brains which is part of P.A.I.N. Prevent Abuse in Neighborhoods to give ladies confidence to overcome and move on.

10 BETH

Beth Rengel is an engaging author and speaker who has had a colorful and interesting history in the spotlight.
As the author of Anchored in Illusion, Beth is very candid about her successes and failures in the world of the Miss Texas and Miss America Pageants, to a professional singer, to the early trenches as a reporter in a man's world in television news. Beth's rise to anchorwoman in several states reflects her fierce determination to reach her goals while all the time hiding behind the illusion of perfection. She has struggled with her own insecurities: her body image, loneliness, the struggle with perfection and the shame of one being fired.

She grew up in Texas and was told by her father before she graduated from high school to: get a job, get married or get a scholarship. She did just that but not in that order. She attended Texas Christian University in Fort Worth, was Miss Texas, third runner up in the Miss America Pageant, was a singer and dancer with the USO troupe, lead singer with the New Christi Minstrels and them pursued a career in broadcast journalism where she was recently inducted into the Oklahoma Pioneer Women in Broadcast Journalism.

Beth has always been an advocate for women who have been bullied, a victim of domestic violence to the strife of men and women forgotten in the nursing homes across our country. Beth's message to each and everyone is to never give up and to believe in their dreams by taking risks. As she lived by her grandmother's words, "you don't regret the things you do, but the things you don't do." It's never too late to reinvent yourself as long as you believe in yourself.

She gives you a road map to examine your own illusions of perfection and to see behind the masks we all wear. Follow your dreams wherever they take you but don't get caught up in the illusions of life.

Chapter 1
Excerpt   My Most Embarrassing Moment

Oh my gosh. I said what?...a little voice screamed inside my head. My heart was in my throat. What have I done? I thought, closing my eyes for a moment as the awful realization washed over me. It had been an accident after sitting on the new set during a live hour newscast. My microphone didn't work for an unbearable half hour. I sat there until the audio man got a mic to me that worked. But when it was my turn to speak, all monitors went to black which technically means we were off the air. Then, there was the fateful slip of the tongue...a curse word. What I said to myself went live over the air. My mic was the only hot microphone. The rest of the story is about being publicly fired and living through the most humiliating time of my life. At that point, you can Give In, Give Up, or Get Back Up.

Chapter 4
Excerpt   The Pleasures of a Ding Dong

I always thought pageants were fun unless you were the one in them. The whole concept of trying to be perfect was a breeding ground for this kind of thinking.Like the watch commercial back in the day said,"You can't be too thin or too tan." That was the mantra preparing for the Miss America Pageant as Miss Texas. Every day started with a poached egg, to the gym for a hard workout, on to the voice coach for an hour, back to the yard to tan in the sun with a slice of tomato on a cup of cottage cheese for lunch.

It was everyday of trying to create that perfect body. By the time dinner was ready, I sat at the table looking and smelling chicken fried steak, mashed potatoes, corn and green beans. But looking up at me was my plate with a pathetic boiled chicken breast on a wilted green leaf of lettuce. I went to bed every night hungry.

But after everyone had gone to bed and I knew the parents and kids were asleep, I was on a mission. I knew where they hid the Ding Dongs. If you're not familiar with the pleasures of a Ding Dong, let me describe these delicious, mouthwatering little chocolate cakes rolled over a creamy white icing center, and they're positively sinful, especially if you're trying to win a beauty pageant. I tiptoed through the kitchen crouching down like a jewel thief in front of the cabinet reaching my arm as far back until I felt my prize of the day...my Ding Dong. After scampering back to my bed and flinging the sheets over my head, I would devour that Ding Dong and then, my tummy was full and I could sleep like a baby.

How did that journey of trying to create the illusion of the perfect body leave me?

Chapter 5
Excerpt   Tall + Dark + Handsome-Love

My entire life I lived by the rules and was literally told how to walk, talk, wear my hair and what to think. During the reign as Miss Texas I was at a ribbon cutting ceremony with some of the Dallas Cowboys football team. I became friends with Defensive End Larry Cole. Larry wanted me to meet his friend, Mike Rengel from college, who played for the New Orleans Saints. He was tall, dark and very handsome. There was only one problem: I didn't love him. We dated long distance while I traveled to Europe on the USO Tour. We dated long distance when I sang with the New Christi Minstrels. When I quit the grueling schedule of singing in every state with the Minstrels, Mike met me with an engagement (ring) and asked me to marry him.

In a perfect world, some romantics might think this was the beginning of the end of my story-a happy ending. After all, I thought being a wife and mother was all I'd ever wanted. That had been my goal growing up. I had never thought of being on TV for a living. I never thought I had it in me. I just wanted to have three kids and drive a station wagon.

It was the perfect fairy tale: I was the good girl, and I had met a good man. We would live happily ever after, of course. that was what I wanted, wasn't it? I didn't want to shatter the illusion.

Chapter 9
Excerpt   Oprah

Oprah glided through the big double doors of Harpo Studios as if she were walking on air. As she approached, the vibrations in the room immediately changed, and things felt different. It was electric.

Her entourage of some eight employees surrounded her like a flock of geese flying V-shaped high in the sky, following their leader. Her hairdresser, makeup artist, producer, writers-together they radiated great respect and created a protective cushion around her.

By this point in my career, I had seen many public figures and done many interviews, yet my heart was pounding with awe. I tried to appear cool, though I felt I was standing before royalty. Oprah Winfrey! I was and still am a huge fan.

the interview lasted about thirty minutes. As we were wrapping up, Oprah asked me, "How are you? What's going on with you?" Her simple yet candid question caught me totally off guard.

Chapter 10
Excerpt   Domestic Violence

Next thing I knew, I was on the floor. My husband had backhanded me in the face-hard. I pulled myself up into a sitting position, already crying. It had hurt-both my cheek and my feelings-and I was frightened because this had come from someone I loved in a home I had pretended was happy. Suddenly, I realized I had been in total denial, all too willing to believe my own illusion of the happy home. He had pushed and shoved me before, but this was the first time he had hit me, and it would be the last. My life changed in an instant. I

knew this marriage was over.
I've often said, "I've had coffee breaks last longer than my last marriage." Until that moment, I had never experienced domestic violence."I'm not a victim," I told myself over and over as he retreated upstairs to the bedroom cursing with anger.

The truth is, women who face domestic violence are all around us in this country. Another misconception is that abuse can only be physical. Both physical and verbal abuse have a direct correlation to a woman's sense of worth.

My daughter had already moved out because of his verbal abuse. I had quit my longtime career as an anchor. I left the big mansion behind and got out and left even without a car.

It was a hard financial adjustment, and it was hard to overcome another feeling of failure. In hindsight, though, it was the most empowering time of my life. I wasn't going to give in or give up. It was time to get back up and reinvent myself. It was just another illusion of what I thought the perfect family in the perfect house looked like.

From Beth:
Finally, don't get caught up in the illusions of life. Life isn't always fair. A perfect body, a perfect childhood, a perfect career, a perfect family-none of these are attainable. They are simply images we try on for size and if we are wise enough, discard before it's too late. Get beyond these illusions, and you'll see that we are all connected. You'll be free to develop a truer vision of yourself and your life.

Beth Rengal and Oprah Winfrey

Beth and Patty Met through Carol Collins-Matza at a book signing for Beth at Victoria's Tea Room in Tulsa Okla. Beth also came and spoke at the kick off for U Can 2 movement at Hard Rock Dallas.

ABOUT THE AUTHOR

Patty McCall

Greetings! I am Patty McCall, Founder and C.E.O. of the P.A.I.N. Foundation. (Prevent Abuse In Neighborhoods.) You may recall my first book *"Unmasking the PAIN Within"* which encompasses my life story of overcoming an abusive relationship. Let's recap a little on that story so you can understand my purpose for our Campaign we are promoting now. This book will tell the stories of just a few women and men that I have met throughout my journey of hope and healing, while overcoming the cycle of abuse that so entrapped my life for many years.

On the outside, my family appeared to have the American dream. Behind the closed doors of our eight acre estate were broken promises, lies, and deception. At that time, I was a devoted wife and loving mother of three that kept the pain within from her children and hid the shame of abuse from the small town we lived in. This is also where my husband had grown up. Through my courage and spiritual guidance, I maintained a convincing mask of peace for the world to see. The verbal abuse and the bruises relayed a different story as I silently suffered on the inside, afraid to unmask the true situation to anyone else. Even the people closest to me did not even know the whole spectrum of the abusive situation I was suffering from.

Today, I am very passionate about reaching others who are afraid to speak out. Maybe by some chance, if you are suffering from abuse or pain of any kind, you may be able to relate to some of the stories within this book and derive the courage to come out of that cycle and receive hope and healing also, just as we all did. I want you to know that you are NOT alone! The stories of the men and women in this book reflect the fact that there is, indeed, light at the end of the tunnel for those who can muster up the courage to step out of their abusive cycles.

After my escape and divorce, I left as far away from Oklahoma as I could. This led me to Hollywood, California. Although many opportunities opened up for me, the pain of the past still haunts me in the midnight hours. I would wake up in a panic, unable to go back to sleep until I journaled these events of the past and feelings of rejection, fear, panic, and anxiety in my little book I kept at my bedside. This journal ended up to be, for me, part of a major healing process and the beginning of my journey to forgiveness. Now with my speaking engagements, I encourage people to write their feelings out on the purple masks that I hand out to them at the end of each presentation. The inspiration I obtained to move on came from a foundational truth of asking God into my heart when I was six years old. He was my best friend, and He is the One who also walked with me through this difficult time. The first foundational scripture that was ingrained into my life was John 3:16. *"For God so loved the world that He gave His only begotten Son, that whosoever believes in Him shall not perish, but have everlasting life."* Had it not been for God, I probably would have had an emotional breakdown. He is the key Being in my recovery process. He is the One who has shown me my purpose in life. Another key inspirational scripture that has pulled me through the hard times is found in Psalms 91, Contemporary English Version: *"Live under the protection of God Most High and stay in the shadow of God all powerful. Then you will say to the Lord, "You are my fortress, my place of safety; you are my God, and I trust you."* Never forget where you dwell in God's kingdom.

Daily devotional time is still an integral part of my recovery process. Recovery doesn't happen overnight; at least it didn't for me. It took me at least five years to be able to speak to people about my previous circumstances of abuse without tears streaming down my face. My advice to you is to be patient with yourself. There's going to be ups and downs in your healing process. I cannot stress the fact enough that daily prayer is going to be a wonderful and necessary part of your journey to recovery. Also, surround yourself with others stronger than yourself who are able to help you and mentor you spiritually and emotionally.

Patty when she accepted Jesus into her heart!

Deborah Perrin Segura, Patty McCall, Ana Figueredo Stuart at Lip sense ribbon cutting. I want to thank these 2 ladies for helping us make a difference in ladies lives.

THE P.A.I.N. FOUNDATION PRESENTS
(PREVENT ABUSE IN NEIGHBORHOODS)

U CAN 2! EVENT

Unmasking the Pain
Overcomer's Unite for a Night of Inspirational Word and Song

SUNDAY, OCTOBER 1ST · 3-7 PM

PATTY MCCALL
P.A.I.N. FOUNDATION
U CAN 2!
FOUNDER AND CEO

DEA MCDANIEL CALDWELL
DALLAS DIRECTOR
AND PRESIDENT
P.A.I.N. FOUNDATION

2211 N Houston Street
Dallas, Texas

BETH RENGEL
AUTHOR & SPEAKER
"ANCHORED IN
ILLUSION"

LORETTA SMAIL
SINGER
SONGWRITER
SPEAKER

GABRIELLA JASSO
SPEAKER &
ADVOCATE
AGAINST
DOMESTIC &
SEXUAL ABUSE

RACHEL JACKSON
SINGER
SONGWRITER
SPEAKER

JANET GALE
SINGER
SONGWRITER
U CAN 2!

Against Domestic Violence

AMERICAN IDOL HOPEFULS

BILLIE JO
SEWELL

KENEDEE
RITTENHOUSE

ANNA
MASSEY

Silent auction - Raffle Drawing - Door Prizes

Admission is **$10** at the door   Full menu available

For more information contact
(469) 569-2408 or (323) 403-3444
www.unmaskingthepainwithin.com

Please go to loveisrespect.org for many resources.

There is hope after so much PAIN! 10 years after my 1st book I jus
attended my youngest daughters wedding. The most preciou
human beings in my life are my 3 children and 3 grandchildren. I ar
extremely proud of each of them.

Billie Jo Sewell, Patty McCall, Kenedee Rittenhouse--American Idol Hopefuls. Kenedee is recording a song "Little Boy" for P.A.I.N. It is written by Janet Gale and will have a Domestic Violence Awareness theme for the music video.

Made in the USA
Coppell, TX
25 August 2023